# Hector BERLIOZ

# ROMÉO ET JULIETTE

*Symphonie damatique*

H 79

(1839)

## Vocal Score
Klavierauszug

**SERENISSIMA MUSIC, INC.**

# CONTENTS

## *Première Partie*

1. Introduction ............................................................................ 1
2. Prologue ................................................................................. 8

## *Deuxième Partie*

1. Roméo seul ........................................................................... 41
2. Nuit sereine ........................................................................... 58
3. La Reine Mab (Scherzo) ....................................................... 79

## *Troisième Partie*

1. Convoi funèbre de Juliette .................................................. 96
2. Roméo au tombeau des Capulets ..................................... 110
3. Finale. ................................................................................. 118

# ORCHESTRA

Piccolo, 2 Flutes, 2 Oboes (2nd also English Horn), 2 Clarinets, 4 Bassoons
4 Horns, 2 Cornets, 2 Trumpets, 3 Trombones, Tuba
Timpani, Percussion, 2 Harps
Violin I, Violin II, Viola, Violoncello, Double Bass

Duration: ca. 95 minutes

First performance: November 24, 1839
Paris, Salle du Conservatoire
Vocal soli, Chorus, Orchestra, Hector Berlioz (conductor)

ISBN: 978-1-60874-259-2

This score is a slightly modified unabridged reprint of the score
issued in 1901 by Breitkopf und Härtel, Leipzig, plate V.A. 1845
edited by Charles Malherbe and Felix Eaingartner with a piano reduction
by Richard Kleinmichel. The score has been scaled to fit the present format.

Printed in the USA
First Printing: July 2022

# ROMÉO ET JULIETTE
## H 79

---

### PREMIÈRE PARTIE.
### ERSTER THEIL.    FIRST PART.
### 1. INTRODUCTION.
Combats - Tumulte - Intervention du Prince.
Kämpfe - Tumult - Dazwischenkunft des Fürsten.
Combat - Tumult - Intervention of the Prince.

Hector Berlioz

SERENISSIMA MUSIC, INC.

## 2.

### Prologue.- Prolog.- Prologue.

**a) Récitatif choral.- a) Choral-Recitativ.- a) Choral Recitativo.**

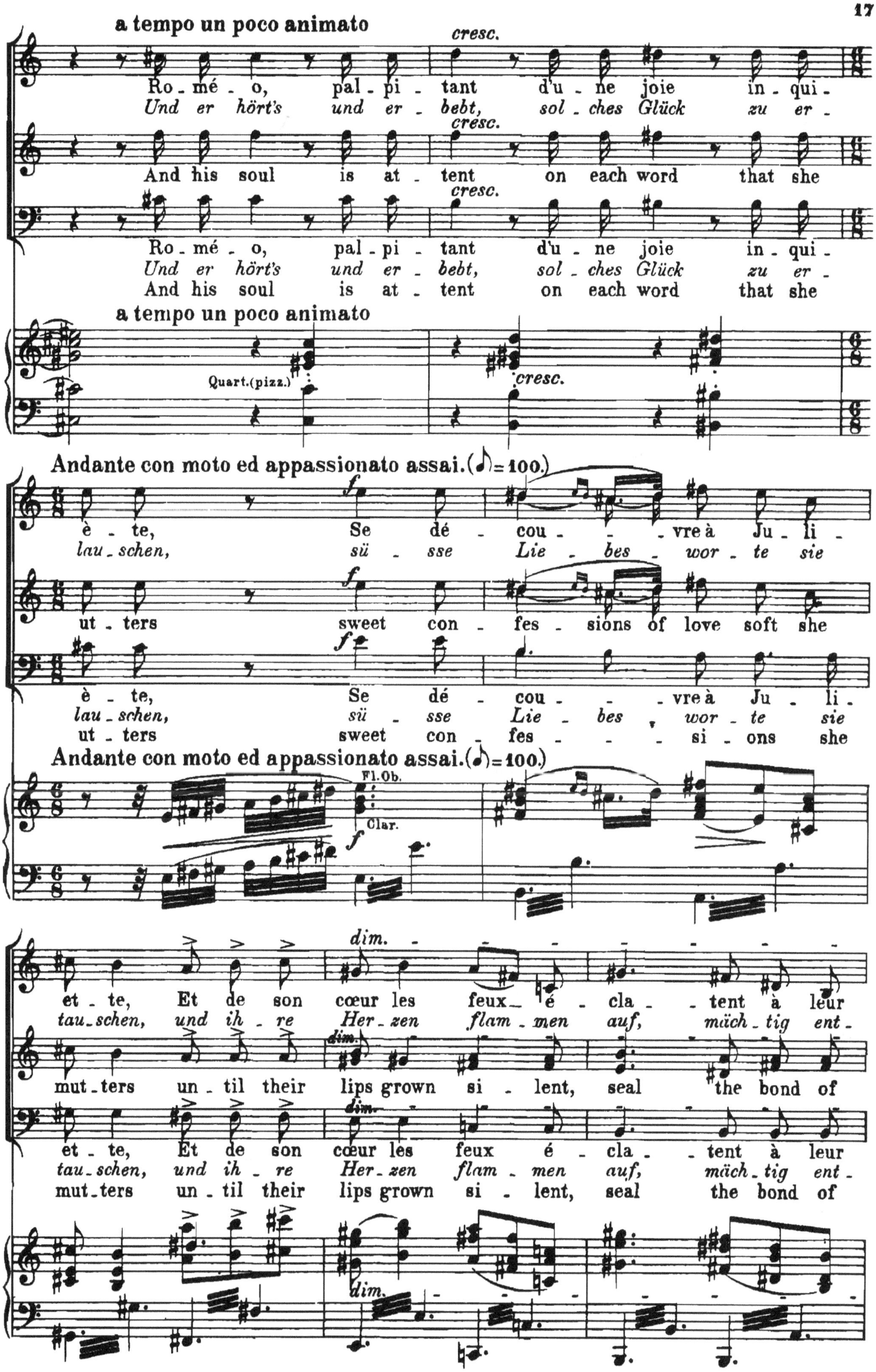
a tempo un poco animato
cresc.
Ro - mé - o, pal - pi - tant d'u - ne joie in - qui -
Und er hört's und er - bebt, sol - ches Glück zu er -
And his soul is at - tent on each word that she
Quart.(pizz.)
Andante con moto ed appassionato assai.(♪=100.)
è - te, Se dé - cou - - vre à Ju - li -
lau - schen, sü - sse Lie - bes - wor - te sie
ut - ters sweet con - fes - sions of love soft she
è - te, Se dé - cou - - - vre à Ju - li -
lau - schen, sü - sse Lie - bes - wor - te sie
ut - ters sweet con - fes - - - si - ons she
Fl.Ob.
Clar.
dim.
et - te, Et de son cœur les feux - é - cla - - tent à leur
tau - schen, und ih - re Her - zen flam - men auf, mäch - tig ent -
mut - ters un - til their lips grown si - lent, seal the bond of
et - te, Et de son cœur les feux é - cla - - tent à leur
tau - schen, und ih - re Her - zen flam - men auf, mäch - tig ent -
mut - ters un - til their lips grown si - lent, seal the bond of

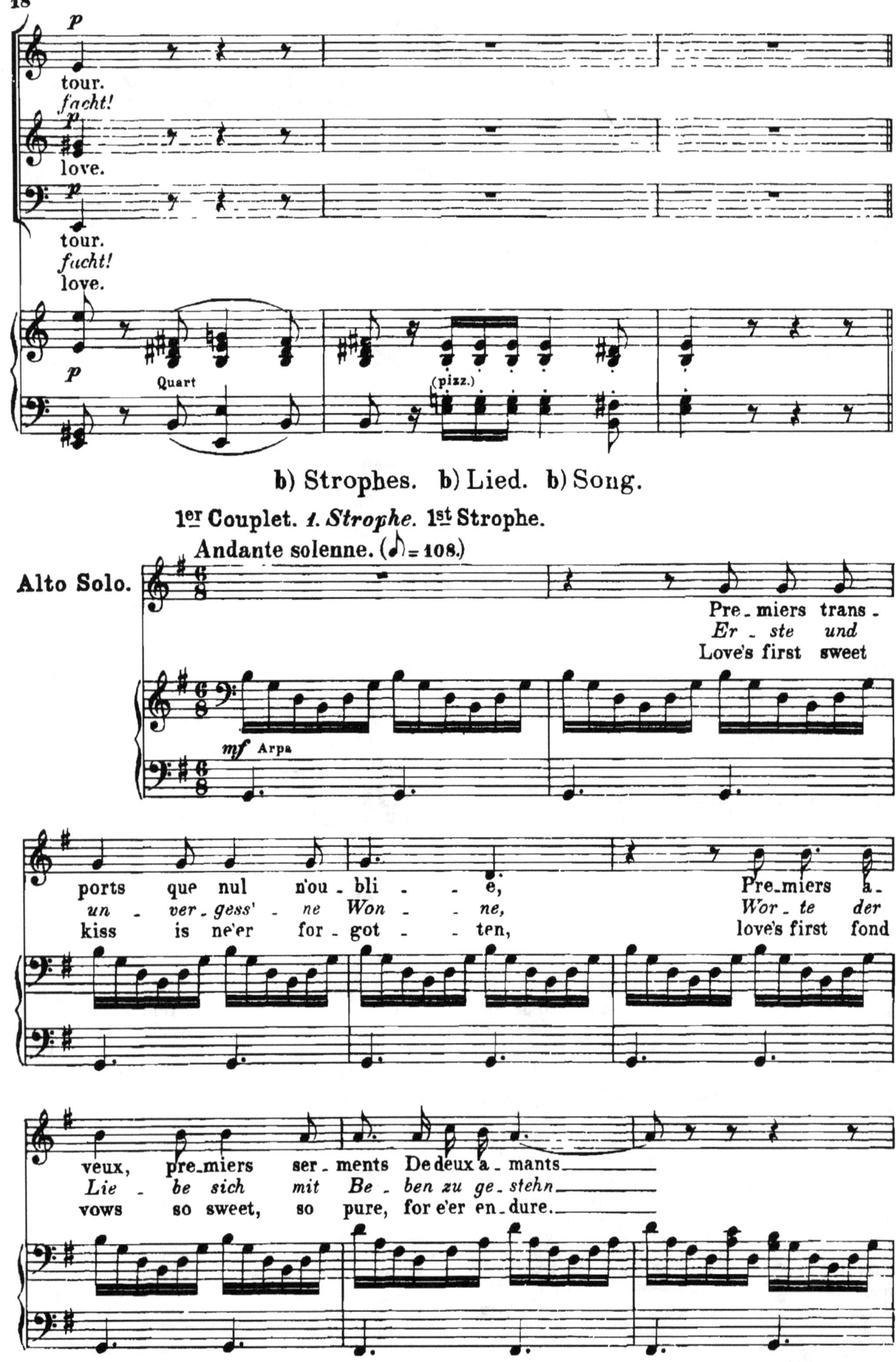

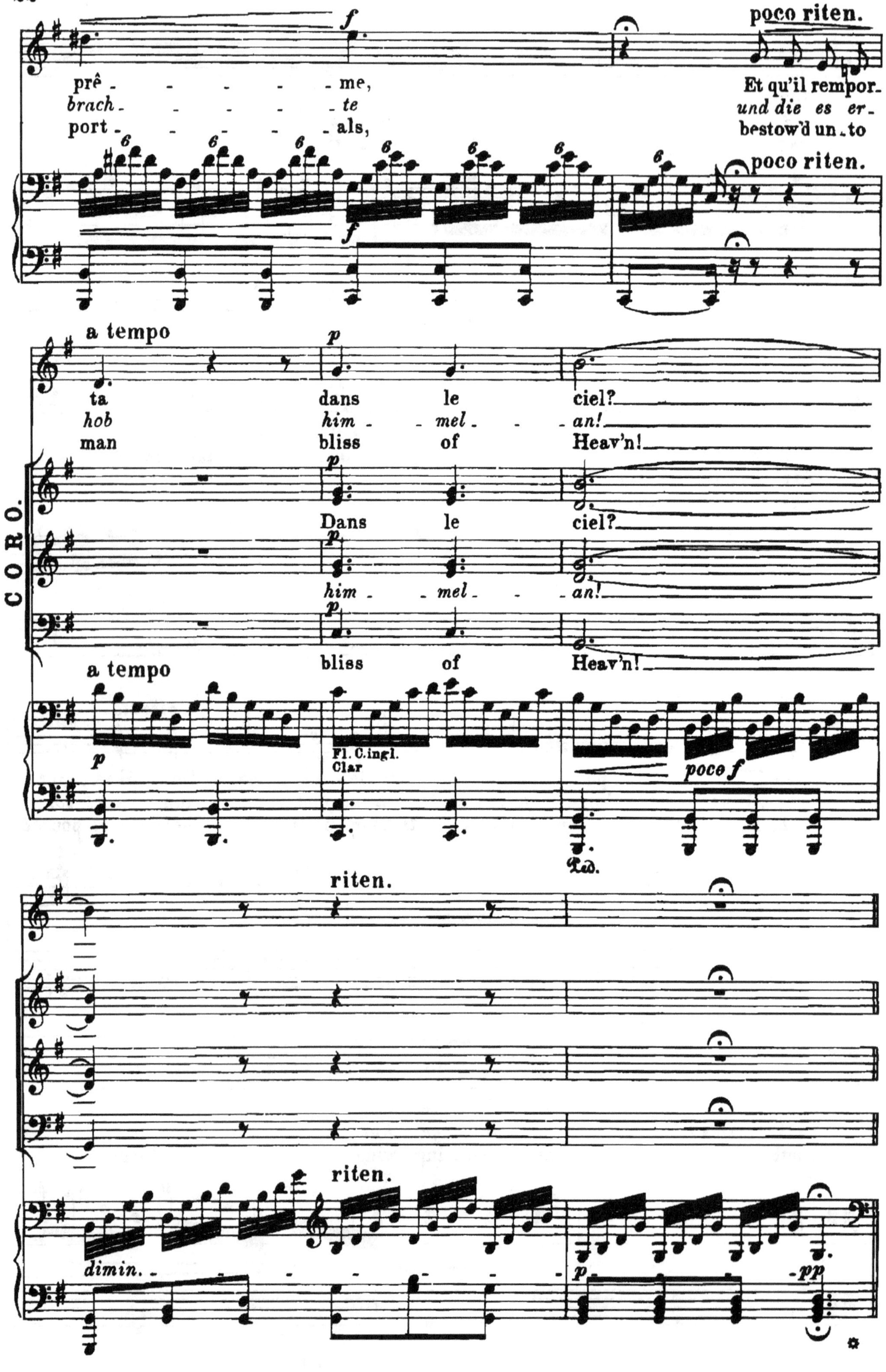

## c) Récitatif et Scherzetto.
## c) Recitativ und Scherzetto.  c) Recitativo and Scherzetto.

# DEUXIÈME PARTIE.
## ZWEITER THEIL.   SECOND PART.
### 1.

Roméo seul - Tristesse - Bruits lointains de Concert et de Bal - Grande Fête chez Capulet.

Romeo allein - Traurigkeit - Entfernte Klänge von Concert und Ball - Grosses Fest bei Capulet.

Romeo alone - Sadness - Distant sounds of Music and dancing - Great festivities in Capulet's Palace.

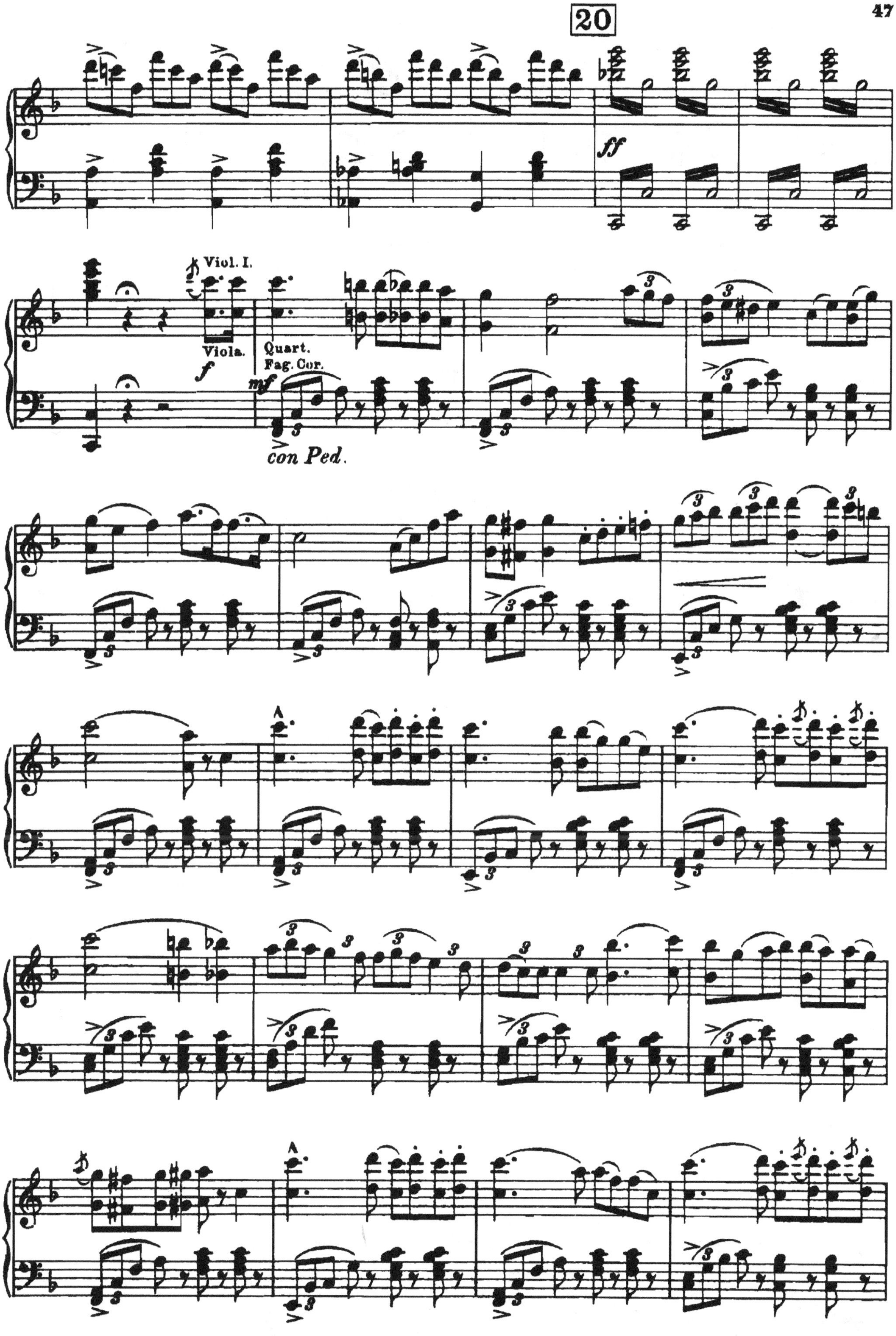
20
ff
Viol. I.
Viola.
f
Quart.
Fag. Cor.
mf
con Ped.

Réunion des deux Thêmes, du Larghetto et de l'Allegro.
*Vereinigung der zwei Themen, des Larghetto und des Allegro.*
The two themes, Larghetto and Allegro combined.

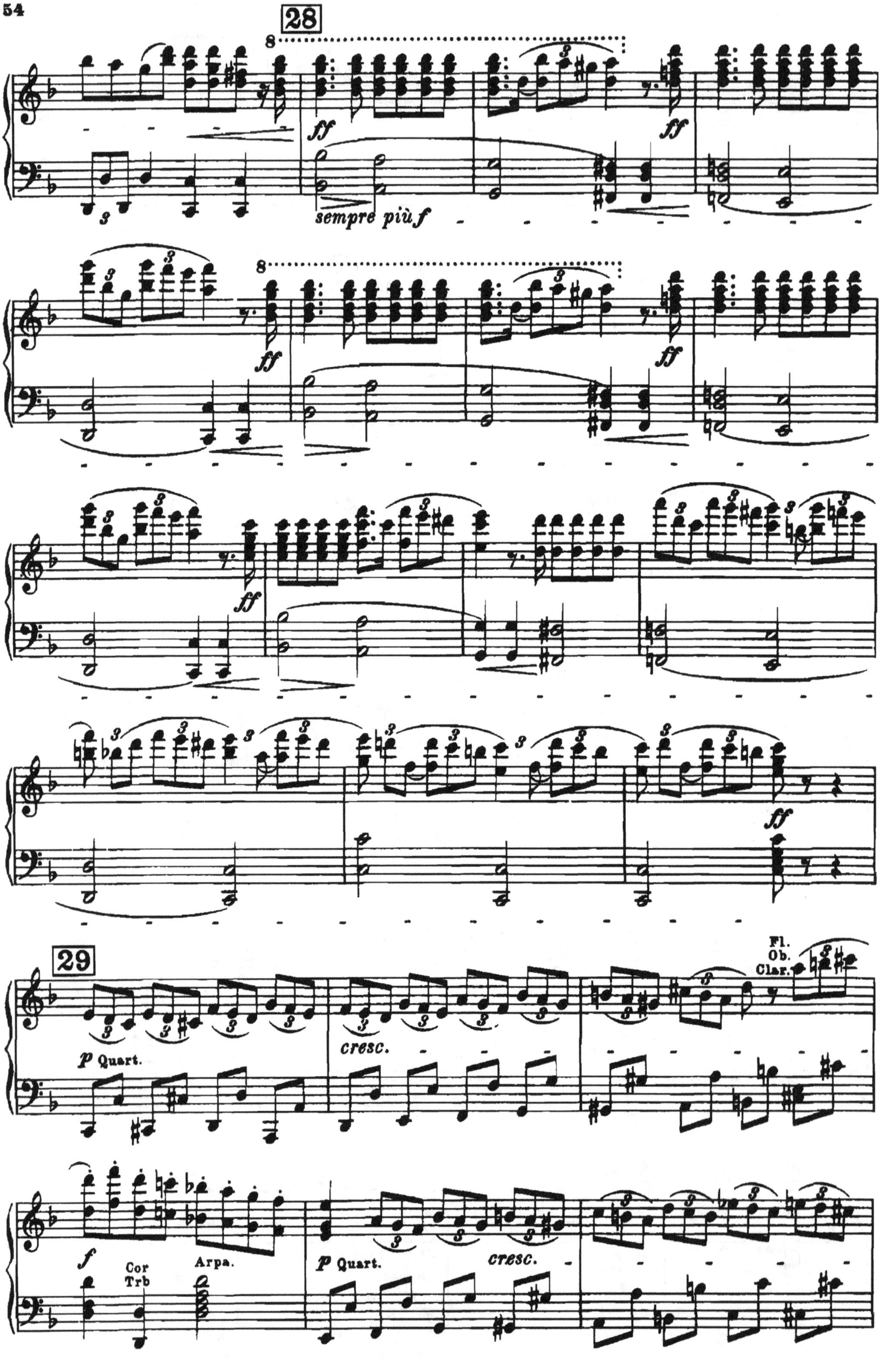
28
sempre più f
ff
29
p Quart.
cresc.
Fl.
Ob.
Clar.
f
Cor
Trb
Arpa.

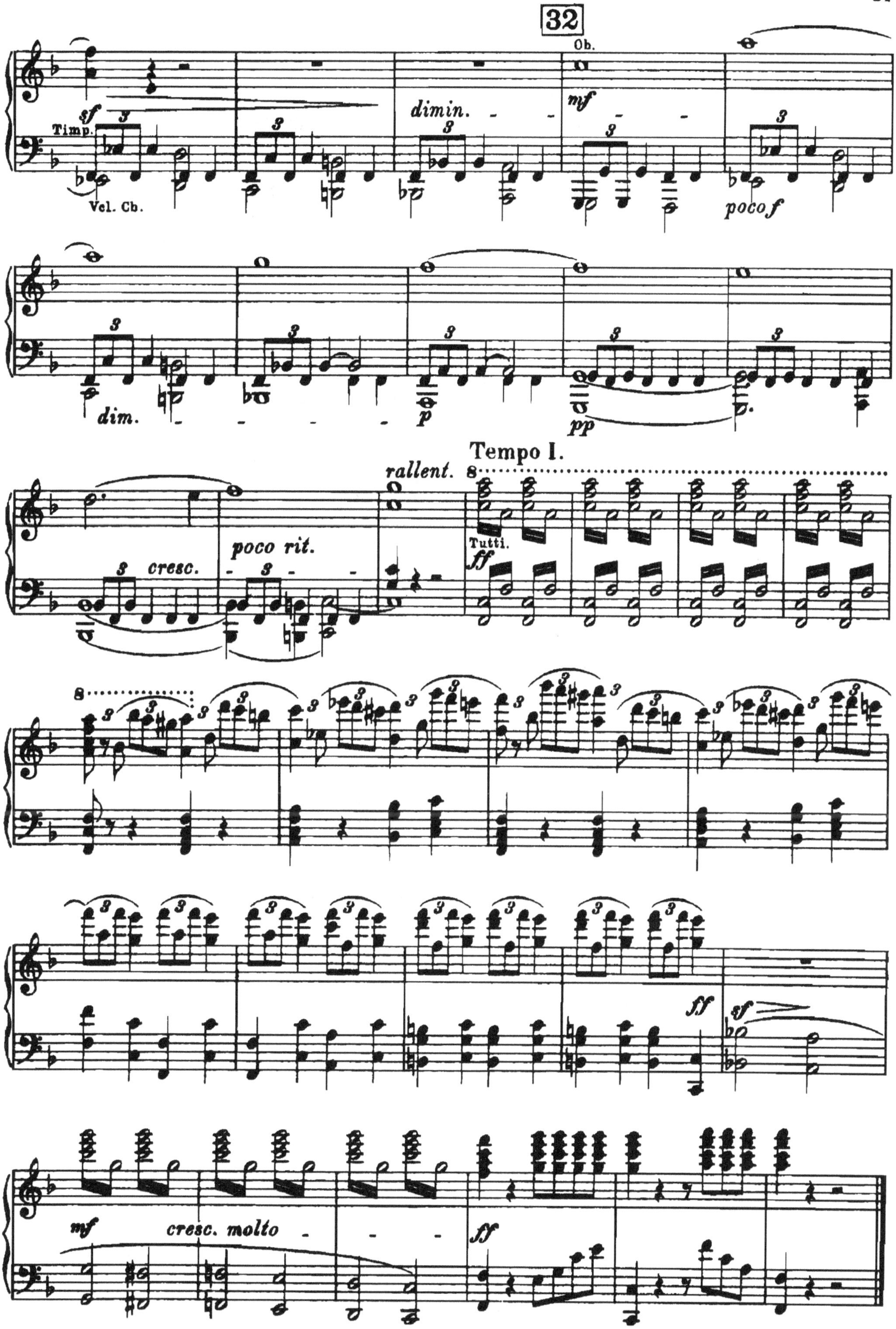
32
Ob.
sf
Timp.
Vel. Cb.
dimin.
mf
poco f
dim.
p
pp
Tempo I.
rallent.
cresc.
poco rit.
Tutti.
ff
sf
mf
cresc. molto
ff

## 2.

**Nuit sereine.— Le Jardin de Capulet silencieux et désert.—
Les jeunes Capulets, sortant de la fête, passent en chantant des
réminiscences de la musique du bal. Scène d'amour.**

**Heitere Nacht.— Der Garten
Capulets, schweigsam und leer.—
Die jungen Capulets verlassen das Fest
und ziehen vorüber, Nachklänge der
Ballmusik singend. Liebesscene.**

**Star-light Night.— Capulet's
Garden, silent and deserted.—
The young Capulets, leaving the hall,
pass by singing fragments of the
dance-music. Love-scene.**

Ce double chœur doit s'exécuter au fond du théâtre, ou dans un salon voisin de l'orchestre si la Symphonie est entendue dans une salle de concert. Il n'est pas nécessaire que le maître de chant puisse voir la mesure du chef d'orchestre; il suffit qu'il puisse entendre la réplique des Cors commençant à la 35ᵉ mesure. Le chef d'orchestre suivra le mouvement du chœur qu'il entendra aisément. Il faut absolument un ou deux instruments, Violons ou Altos, pour donner le ton aux choristes et les empêcher de baisser, les choristes ne pouvant pendant qu'ils chantent rien entendre de l'orchestre qui joue aussi piano que possible.
(Note de H. Berlioz.)

*Dieser Doppelchor muss im Hintergrunde des Theaters, oder, wenn die Symphonie in einem Concertsaal zu Gehör gebracht wird, in einem dem Orchester benachbarten Raume ausgeführt werden! Es ist nicht nothwendig, dass der Chormeister den Takt des Dirigenten sieht; es genügt, wenn er das Stichwort der Hörner hört, welche im 35. Takt einsetzen. Der Dirigent folgt dem Zeitmaass des Chores, welches er bequem hören kann. Unbedingt müssen 1 oder 2 Instrumente, Violinen oder Bratschen, den Chorsängern den Ton angeben, damit diese nicht zu tief singen, da sie während des Gesanges nichts von dem gänzlich pianissimo spielenden Orchester hören können. (Anmerkung von H. Berlioz.)*

This double-chorus to be sung in the background of the (stage) theatre, or in a room adjoining the orchestra if the symphony be performed in a Concert-hall. The Chorus-master need not see the Orchestral-conductor's bâton; all he requires is to hear the cue given by the horns in the 35th bar where they commence. The Conductor then follows the chorus which he can easily hear. It is absolutely essential that one or two instruments 1st violins or tenor-violins shall give the chorus the pitch, to prevent the latter from getting out of tune, as they cannot hear anything of the orchestra playing pianissimo.
(Berlioz's own Note.)

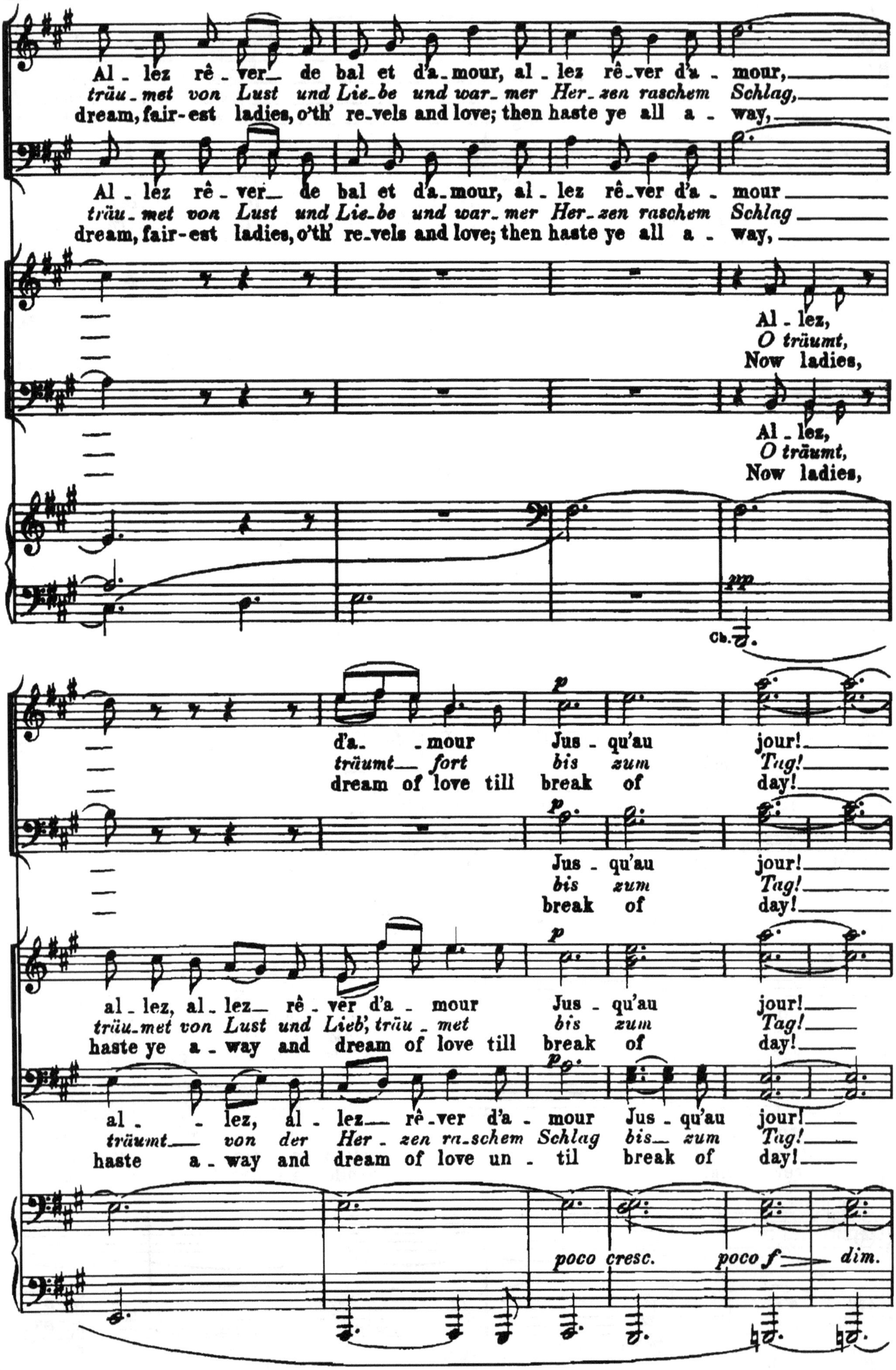
Al - lez rê - ver - de bal et d'a - mour, al - lez rê - ver d'a - mour,
träu - met von Lust und Lie - be und war - mer Her - zen raschem Schlag,
dream, fair - est ladies, o'th' re - vels and love; then haste ye all a - way,
Al - lez rê - ver - de bal et d'a - mour, al - lez rê - ver d'a - mour
träu - met von Lust und Lie - be und war - mer Her - zen raschem Schlag
dream, fair - est ladies, o'th' re - vels and love; then haste ye all a - way,
Al - lez,
O träumt,
Now ladies,
Al - lez,
O träumt,
Now ladies,
pp
Cb.
d'a - mour Jus - qu'au jour!
träumt fort bis zum Tag!
dream of love till break of day!
p
Jus - qu'au jour!
bis zum Tag!
break of day!
p
al - lez, al - lez rê - ver d'a - mour Jus - qu'au jour!
träu - met von Lust und Lieb', träu - met bis zum Tag!
haste ye a - way and dream of love till break of day!
p
al - lez, al - lez rê - ver d'a - mour Jus - qu'au jour!
träumt von der Her - zen ra - schem Schlag bis zum Tag!
haste a - way and dream of love un - til break of day!
poco cresc. poco f dim.

sempre dim.
Ah! Quel - le nuit! Quel fes - tin!
Ah! welch ei - ne Zau - ber - nacht!
Fare - well! the stars shine bright.
sempre dim.
Ah! Quel - le nuit! Quel fes - tin!
Ah! welch ei - ne Zau - ber - nacht!
Fare - well! the stars shine bright.
sempre dim.
Au re - voir! Ah! Quel - le nuit!
Gu - te Nacht! Ah! welch ei - ne
Now, good night! Fare - well! the
sempre dim.
Au re - voir! Au re - voir! Quel - le nuit!
Gu - te Nacht! Gu - te Nacht! welch ei - ne
Now, good night! Now, good night! while the
pp
La bel - le fê - te! Da - mes
Fröh - li - che Gä - ste! träumt vom
dream of the rev - els! while the
ppp
La bel - le fê - te! Da - mes
Fröh - li - che Gä - ste! träumt vom
dream of the rev - els! while the
Quel fes - tin! La bel - le fê - te!
Fes - tes - pracht! träu - met vom Fes - te!
stars shine bright, dream of the rev - els!
Quel fes - tin! La bel - le fê - te!
Fes - tes - pracht! träu - met vom Fes - te!
stars shine bright, dream of the rev - els!

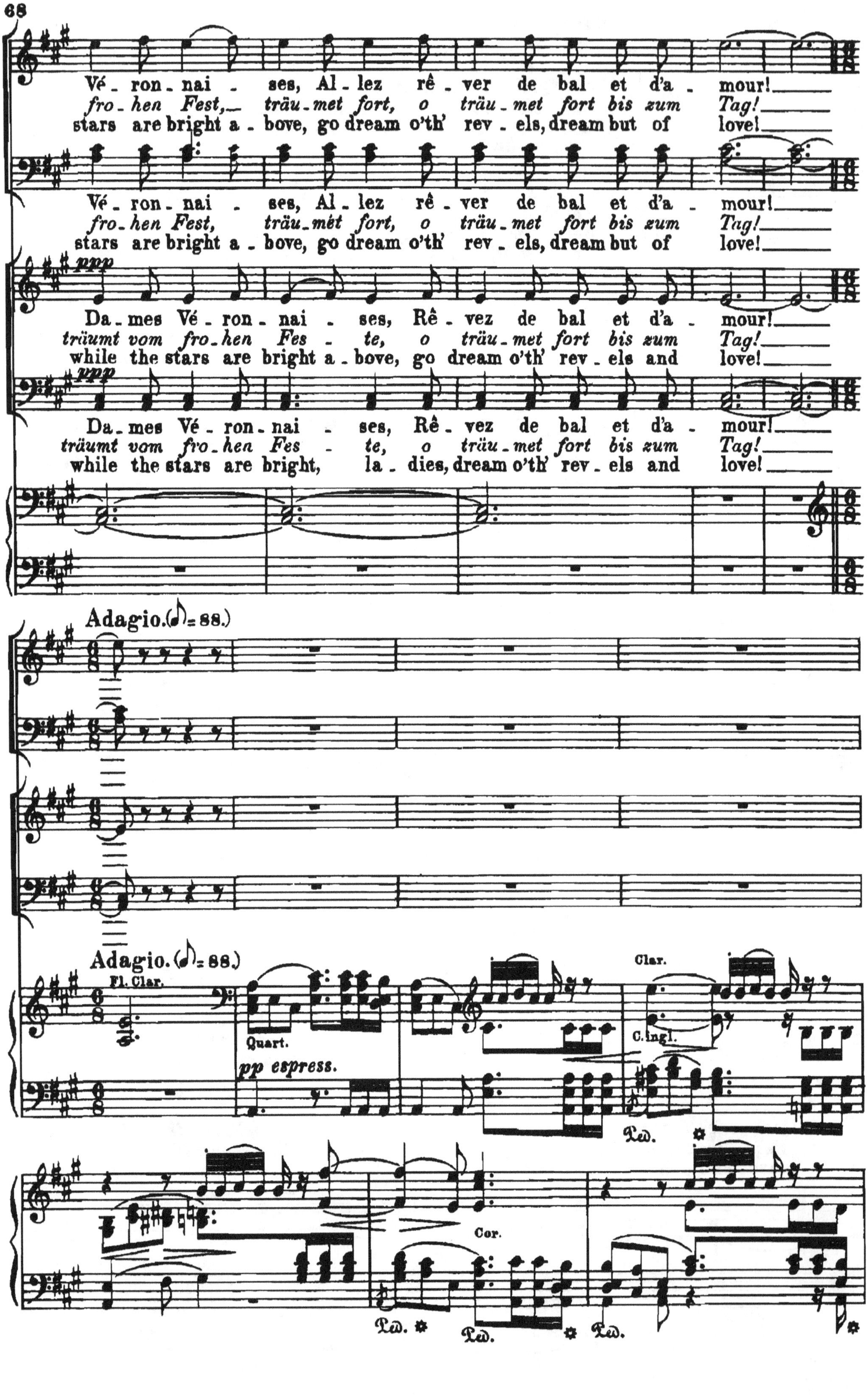
Vé - ron - nai - ses, Al - lez rê - ver de bal et d'a - mour!
fro - hen Fest, träu - met fort, o träu - met fort bis zum Tag!
stars are bright a - bove, go dream o'th' rev - els, dream but of love!
Vé - ron - nai - ses, Al - lez rê - ver de bal et d'a - mour!
fro - hen Fest, träu - mét fort, o träu - met fort bis zum Tag!
stars are bright a - bove, go dream o'th' rev - els, dream but of love!
ppp
Da - mes Vé - ron - nai - ses, Rê - vez de bal et d'a - mour!
träumt vom fro - hen Fes - te, o träu - met fort bis zum Tag!
while the stars are bright a - bove, go dream o'th' rev - els and love!
ppp
Da - mes Vé - ron - nai - ses, Rê - vez de bal et d'a - mour!
träumt vom fro - hen Fes - te, o träu - met fort bis zum Tag!
while the stars are bright, la - dies, dream o'th' rev - els and love!
Adagio. (♪= 88.)
Adagio. (♪= 88.)
Fl. Clar.
Quart.
pp espress.
Clar.
C. ingl.
Cor.

72

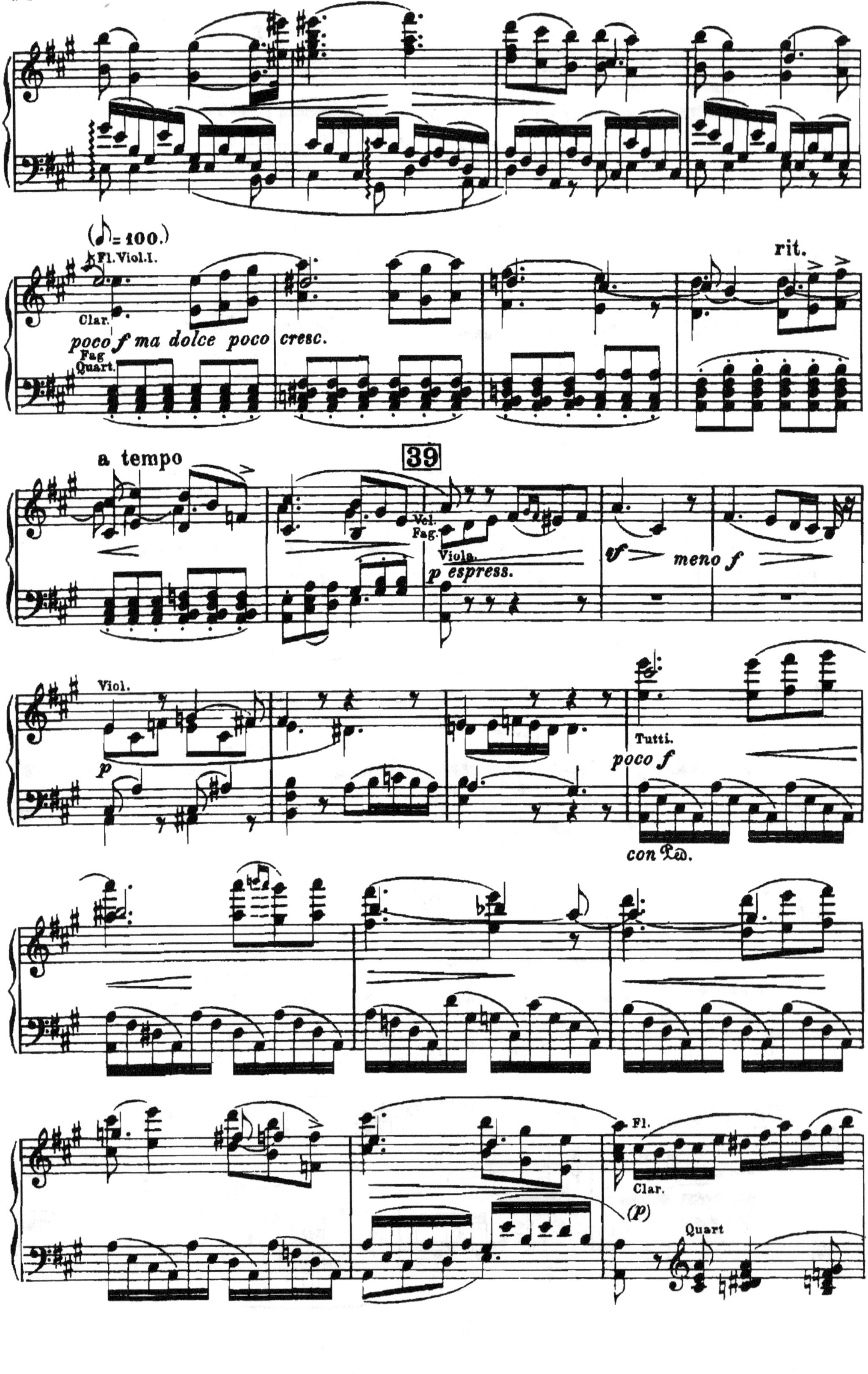
(♪= 100.)
Fl. Viol. I.
Clar.
poco f ma dolce poco cresc.
Fag
Quart.
rit.
a tempo
39
Vcl.
Fag.
Viola
p espress.
sf
meno f
Viol.
p
Tutti.
poco f
con Ped.
Fl.
Clar.
(p)
Quart

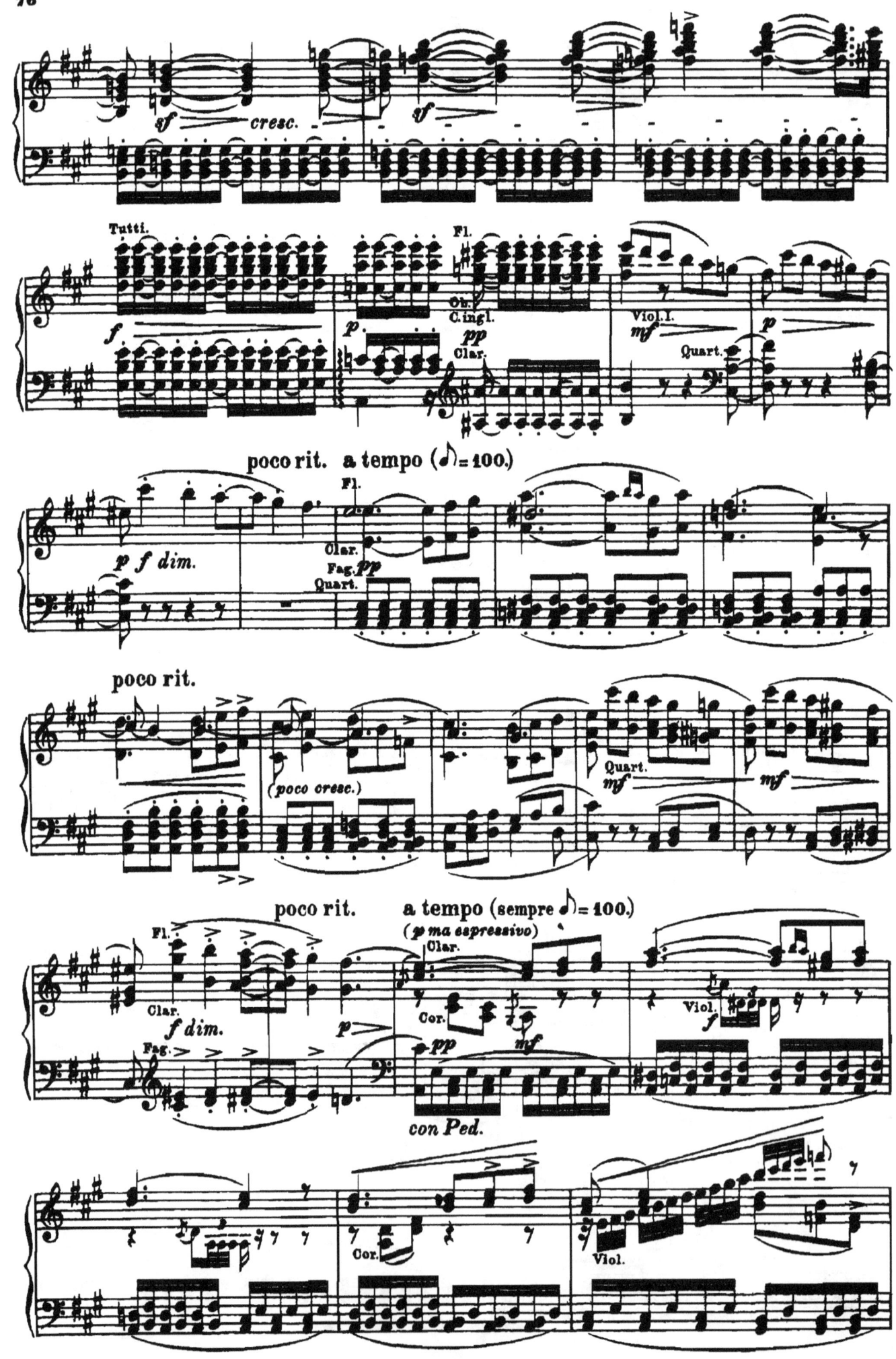

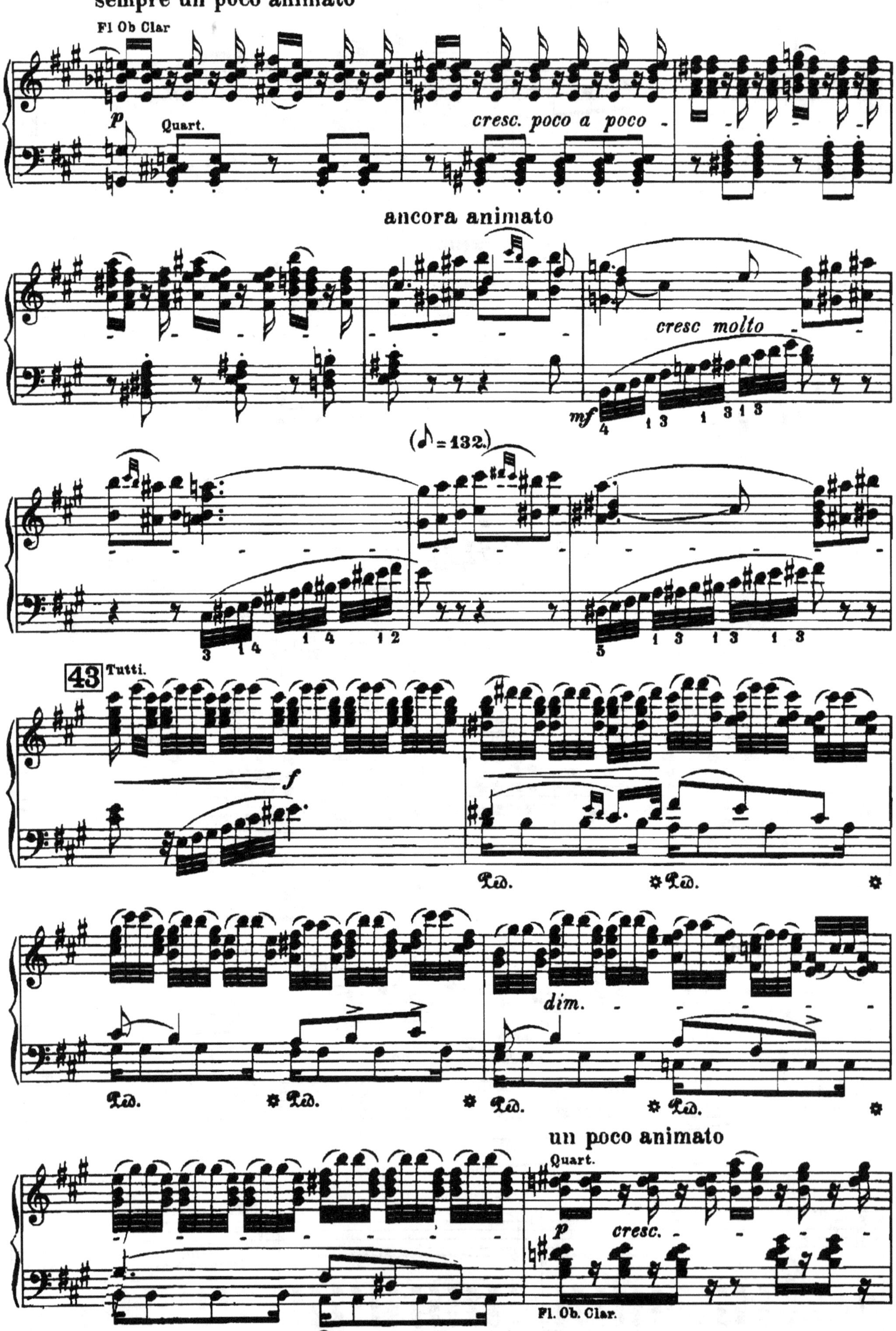
sempre un poco animato
Fl Ob Clar
p
Quart.
cresc. poco a poco
ancora animato
cresc molto
mf
(♪ = 132.)
43
Tutti.
f
dim.
un poco animato
Quart.
p
cresc.
Fl. Ob. Clar.

## 3.

### La Reine Mab ou la Fée des Songes.
Königin Mab oder die Fee der Träume.   Queen Mab or the Fairy of Dreams.

**Scherzo.**

Prestissimo. (♩. = 138.)

82

84

# TROISIÈME PARTIE.
# DRITTER THEIL.    THIRD PART.

## 1.

Convoi Funèbre de Juliette.
Juliens Leichenbegängniss.    Juliet's Funeral.

Marche Fuguée: instrumentale d'abord, avec une psalmodie sur une seule note dans les voix; vocale ensuite, avec la psalmodie dans l'orchestre.
*Zuerst fugirter instrumentaler Marsch mit einer Psalmodie auf einer einzigen Note in den Singstimmen, hierauf vokal mit der Psalmodie im Orchester.*
Fugal March, at first instrumental with a psalmody on one note in the voices; then vocal with the psalmody in the orchestra.

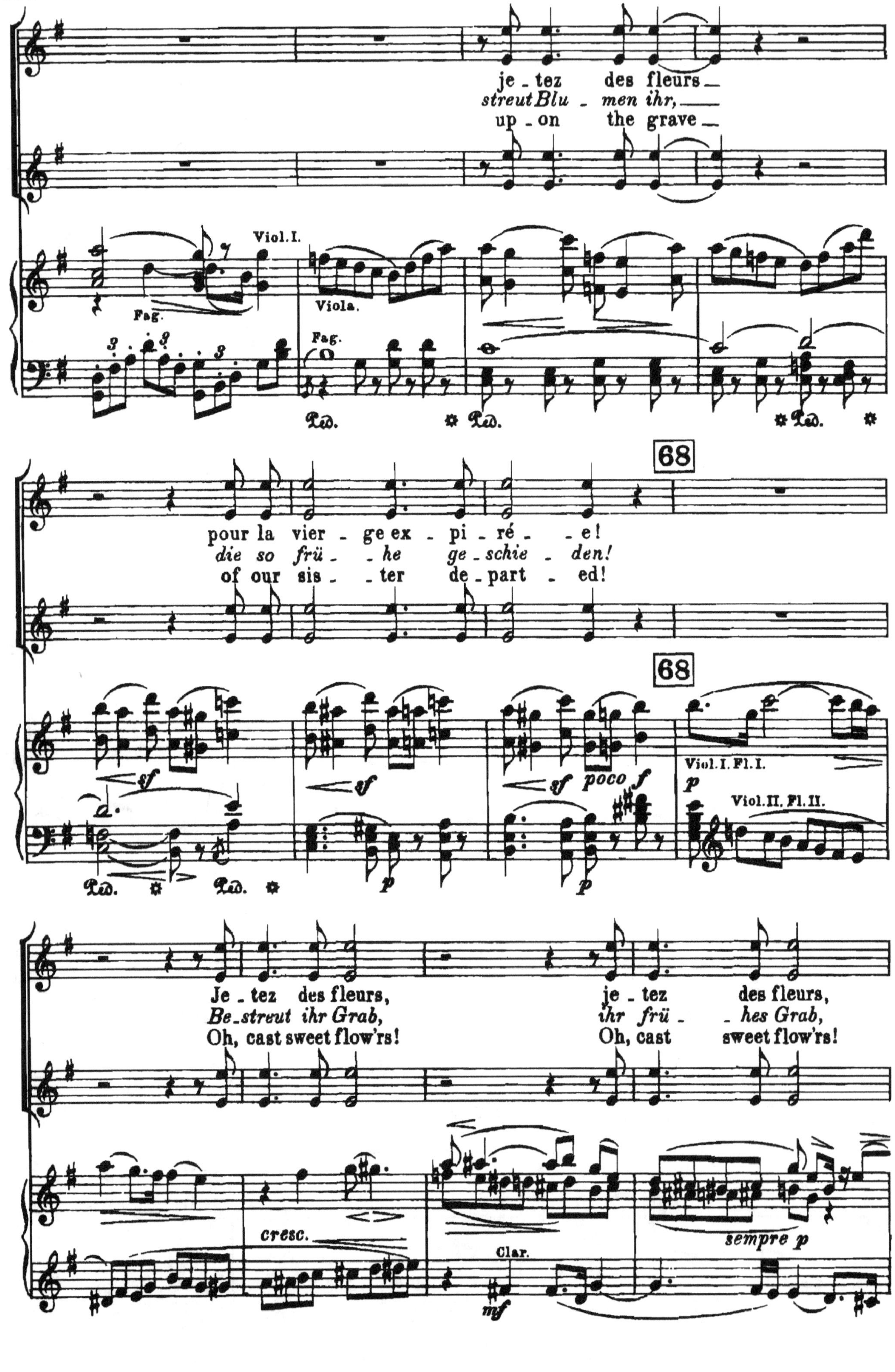
je - tez des fleurs -
streut Blu - men ihr, -
up - on the grave -
Viol. I.
Fag.
Viola.
Fag.
68
pour la vier - ge ex - pi - ré - e!
die so frü - he ge - schie - den!
of our sis - ter de - part - ed!
68
sf
sf
sf
poco f
p
p
Viol. I. Fl. I.
p
Viol. II. Fl. II.
Je - tez des fleurs,
Be - streut ihr Grab,
Oh, cast sweet flow'rs!
je - tez des fleurs,
ihr frü - hes Grab,
Oh, cast sweet flow'rs!
cresc.
Clar.
mf
sempre p

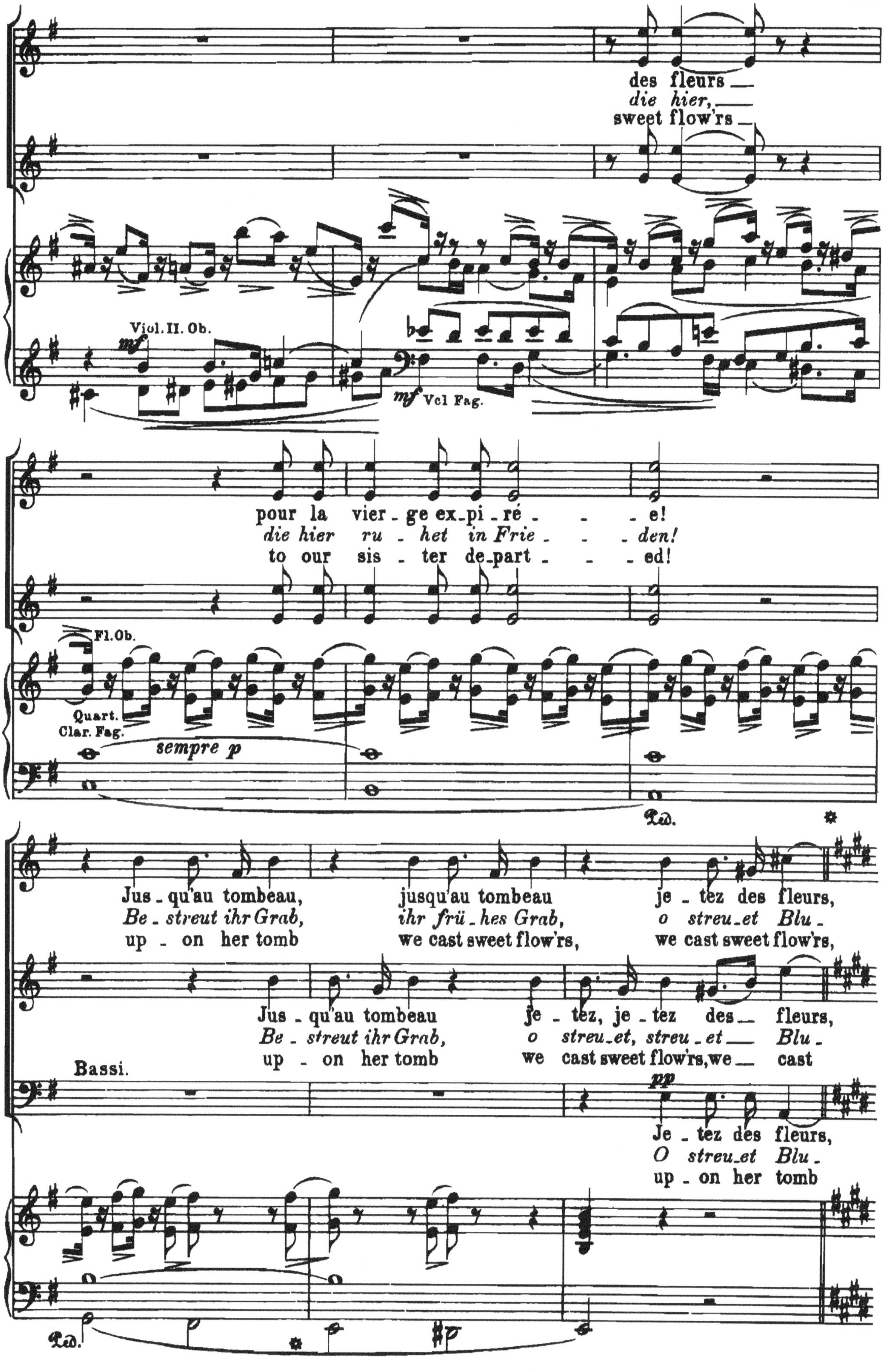
des fleurs
die hier,
sweet flow'rs
Viol. II. Ob.
mf
mf Vcl Fag.
pour la vier - ge ex - pi - ré - - - e!
die hier ru - het in Frie - - - den!
to our sis - ter de - part - - - ed!
Fl. Ob.
Quart.
Clar. Fag.
sempre p
Jus - qu'au tombeau, jusqu'au tombeau je - tez des fleurs,
Be - streut ihr Grab, ihr frü - hes Grab, o streu - et Blu -
up - on her tomb we cast sweet flow'rs, we cast sweet flow'rs,
Jus - qu'au tombeau je - tez, je - tez des fleurs,
Be - streut ihr Grab, o streu - et, streu - et Blu -
up - on her tomb we cast sweet flow'rs, we cast
Bassi.
pp
Je - tez des fleurs,
O streu - et Blu -
up - on her tomb

je - tez des fleurs pour la vier - ge expi - ré - e! Je -
- men auf ihr Grab, die früh von uns ge - schie - den! O
sweet flow'rs to her whom Death from us hath part - ed. We

je - tez des fleurs pour la vier - ge expi - ré - e! Je -
- men auf ihr Grab, die früh von uns ge - schie - den! O
sweet flow'rs to her whom Death from us hath part - ed. We

je - tez des fleurs pour la vier - ge expi - ré - e! Je -
- men auf ihr Grab, die früh von uns ge - schie - den! O
we cast sweet flow'rs whom Death from us hath part - ed. We

tez, je - tez des fleurs pour la vier -
streu - et ihr Blu - - men, der jung - fräu - lich
cast sweet flow'rs, sweet flow'rs, to her whom Death from

tez des fleurs, je - tez des fleurs pour la vier -
naht in Harm, o naht in Harm der Jung - frau
cast sweet flow'rs, sweet flow'rs we cast, to her now from

tez des fleurs, je - tez des fleurs pour la vier -
naht in Harm, o naht in Harm der Jung - frau
cast sweet flow'rs, sweet flow'rs we cast, to her from

## 2.
### Roméo au tombeau des Capulets.
Invocation – Réveil de Juliette. – Joie délirante Désespoir;
dernières angoisses et mort des deux amants.

**Romeo in der Gruft der Capulets.**
Anrufung – Juliens Erwachen. Wahnsinnige Freude, Verzweiflung; Todesangst und Verscheiden der beiden Liebenden.

**Romeo in the family-vault of the Capulets.**
Invocation – Juliet's awakening.
Delirious joy, despair;
Anguish and death of both the lovers.

Invocation.
Anrufung.
Invocation.

### Réveil de Juliette.
### Juliens Erwachen.   Juliet's awakening.

## Joie délirante.
### Wahnsinnige Freude.  Delirious joy.

Allegro vivace ed appassionato assai. (♩=144.)

# Dernières angoisses et mort des deux amants.
## Todesangst und Verscheiden der beiden Liebenden.   Anguish and death of both the lovers.

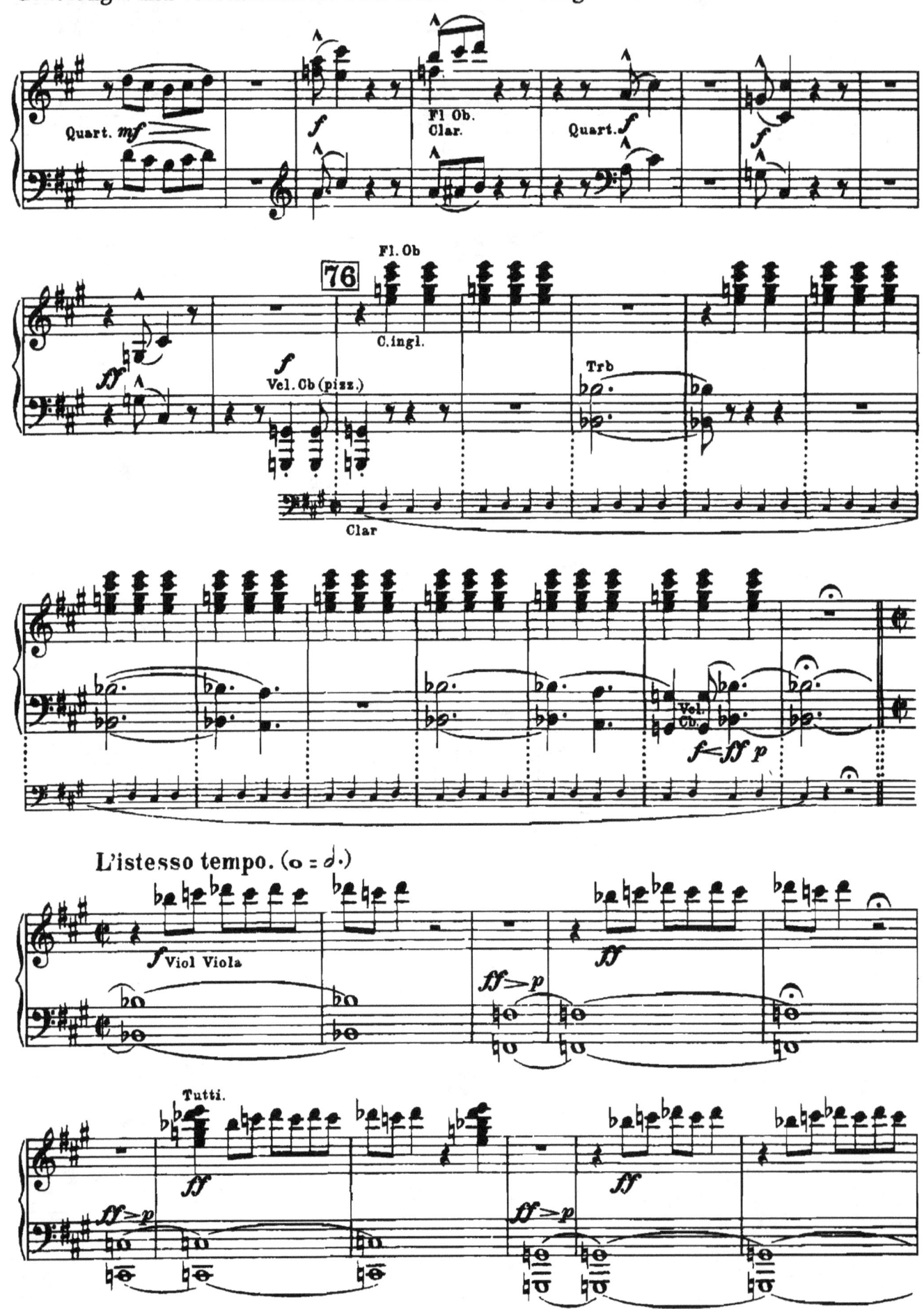

118

# 3.
## Finale.

La foule accourt au Cimetière.- Rixe des Capulets et des Montagus.
Récitatif et Air du Père Laurence.- Serment de Réconciliation.

## Finale.

Die Menge eilt zum Kirchhof.-
Streit der Capulets und Montagus.
Recitativ und Arie des Pater Lorenzo.
Schwur und Versöhnung.

## Finale.

The crowd hastens to the churchyard.-
Dispute between the Capulets and the Montagues.
Recitative and Aria of Friar Laurence.
Oath and Reconciliation.

a) Chœurs et Récitatif du Père Laurence.
a) Chöre und Recitativ des Pater Lorenzo.
a) Chorus and Recitative of Friar Laurence.

## b) Air. b) Arie. b) Aria.

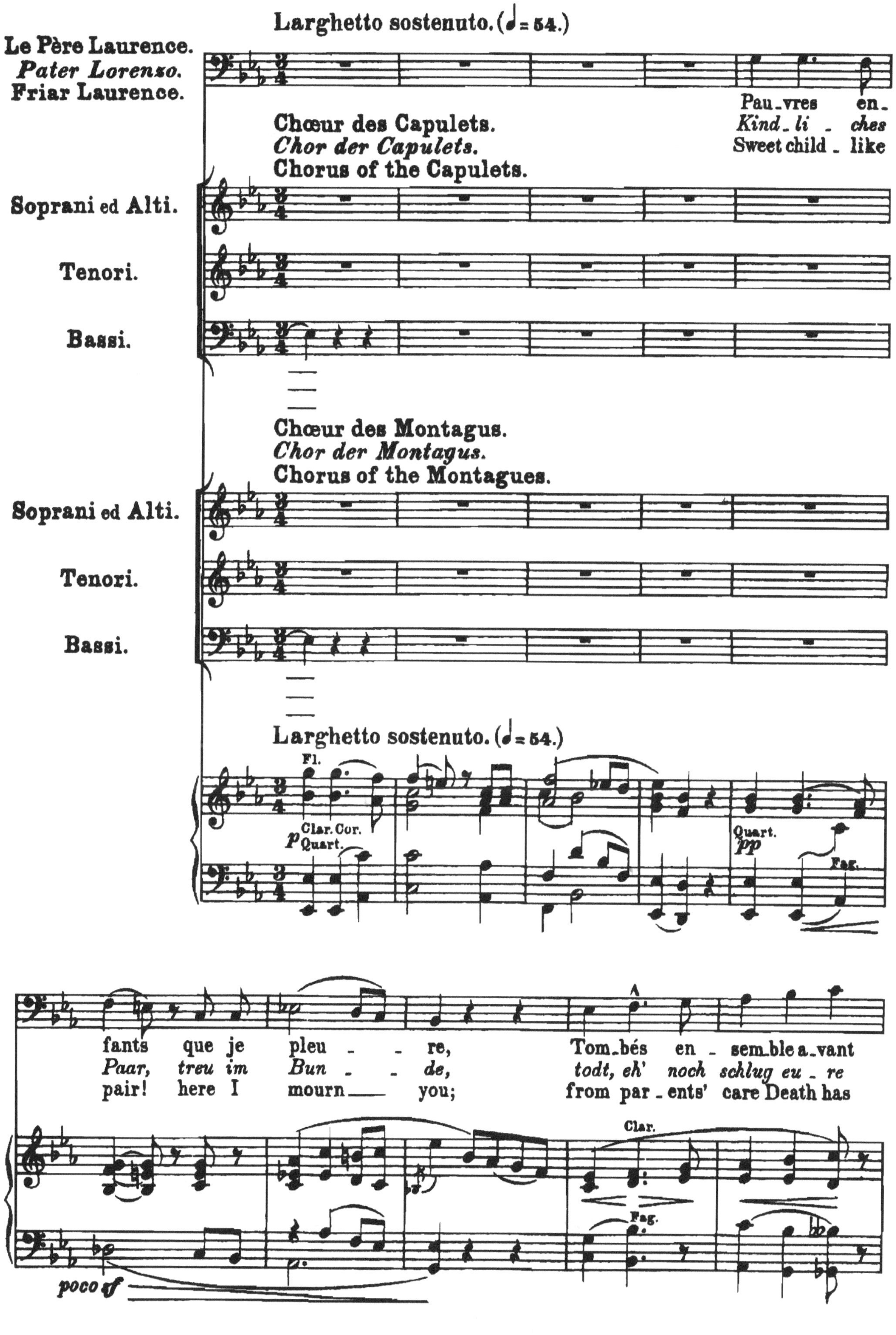
Larghetto sostenuto. (♩= 54.)
Le Père Laurence.
Pater Lorenzo.
Friar Laurence.
Pau_vres en_
Kind_li _ ches
Sweet child _ like
Chœur des Capulets.
Chor der Capulets.
Chorus of the Capulets.
Soprani ed Alti.
Tenori.
Bassi.
Chœur des Montagus.
Chor der Montagus.
Chorus of the Montagues.
Soprani ed Alti.
Tenori.
Bassi.
Larghetto sostenuto. (♩= 54.)
Fl.
Clar. Cor.
p Quart.
Quart.
pp
Fag.
fants que je pleu - - re, Tom_bés en _ sem_ble a_vant
Paar, treu im Bun - - de, todt, eh' noch schlug eu _ re
pair! here I mourn you; from par _ ents' care Death has
Clar.
Fag.
poco sf

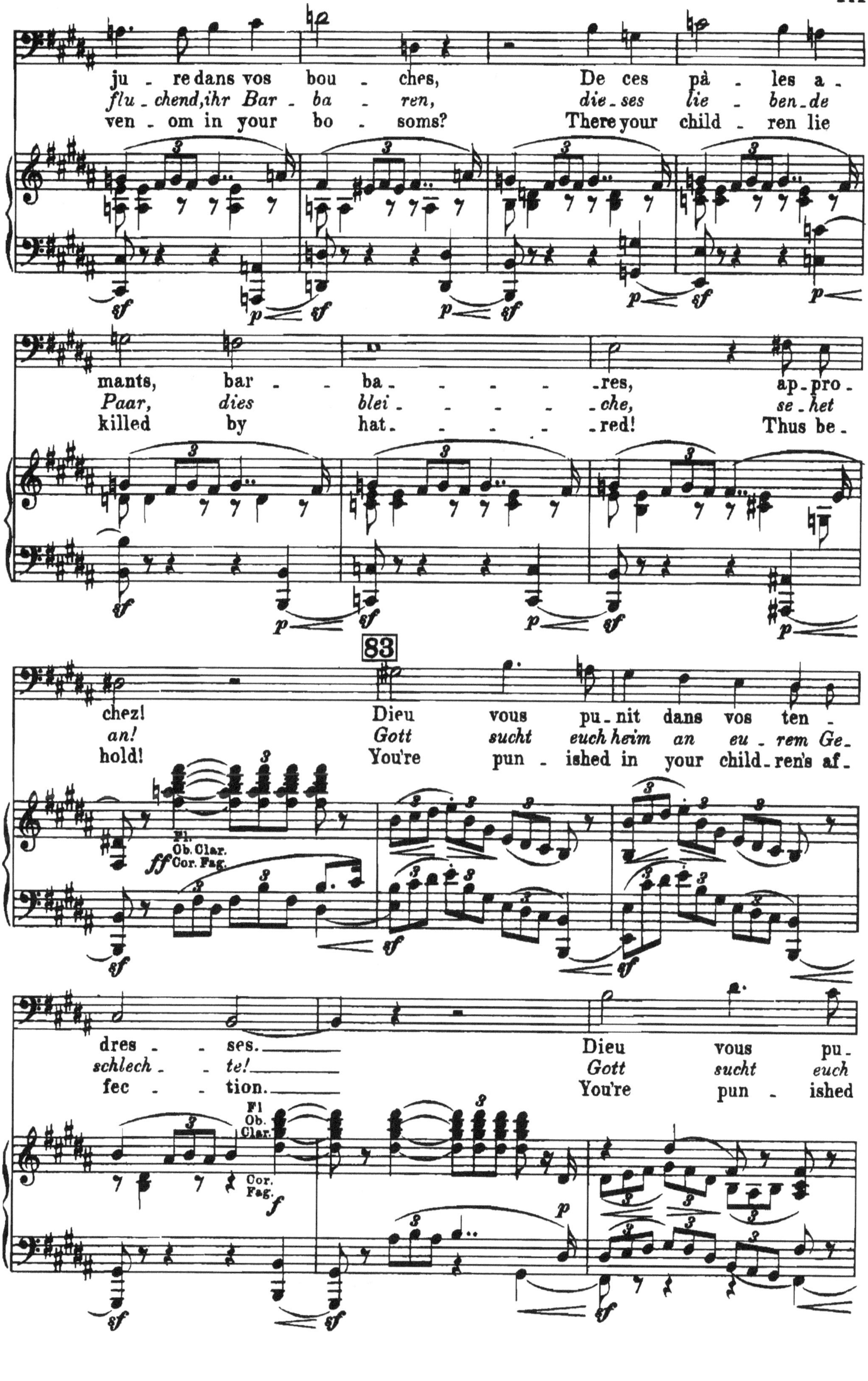
ju - re dans vos bou - ches, De ces pâ - les a -
flu - chend, ihr Bar - ba - ren, die - ses lie - ben - de
ven - om in your bo - soms? There your child - ren lie
mants, bar - - ba - - - - - - res, ap - pro -
Paar, dies blei - - - - - che, se - het
killed by hat - - - - - - red! Thus be -
83
chez! Dieu vous pu - nit dans vos ten -
an! Gott sucht euch heim an eu - rem Ge -
hold! You're pun - ished in your child - ren's af -
Fl. Ob. Clar. Cor. Fag.
dres - ses. Dieu vous pu -
schlech - te! Gott sucht euch
fec - tion. You're pun - ished
Fl Ob. Clar. Cor. Fag.

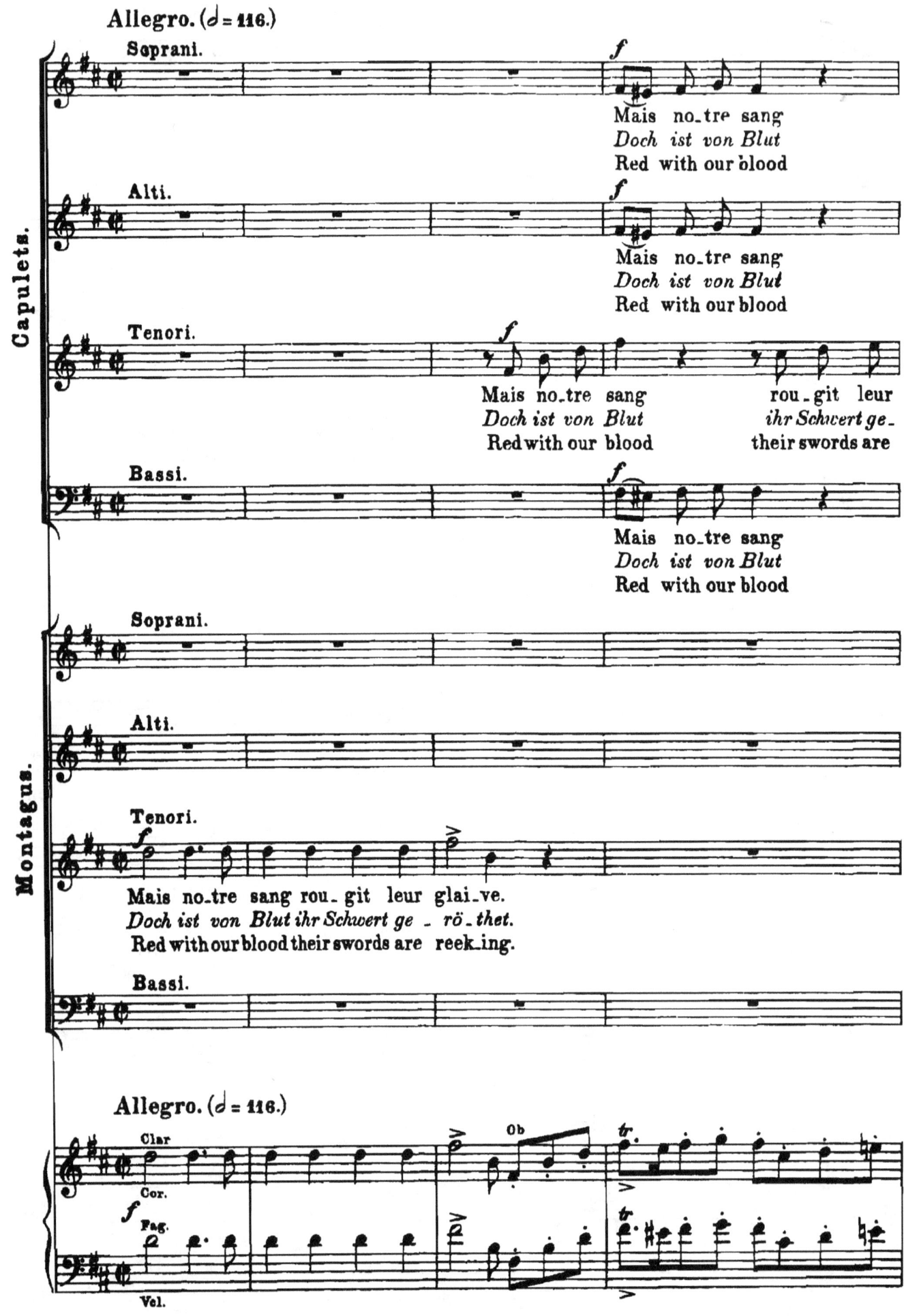

146

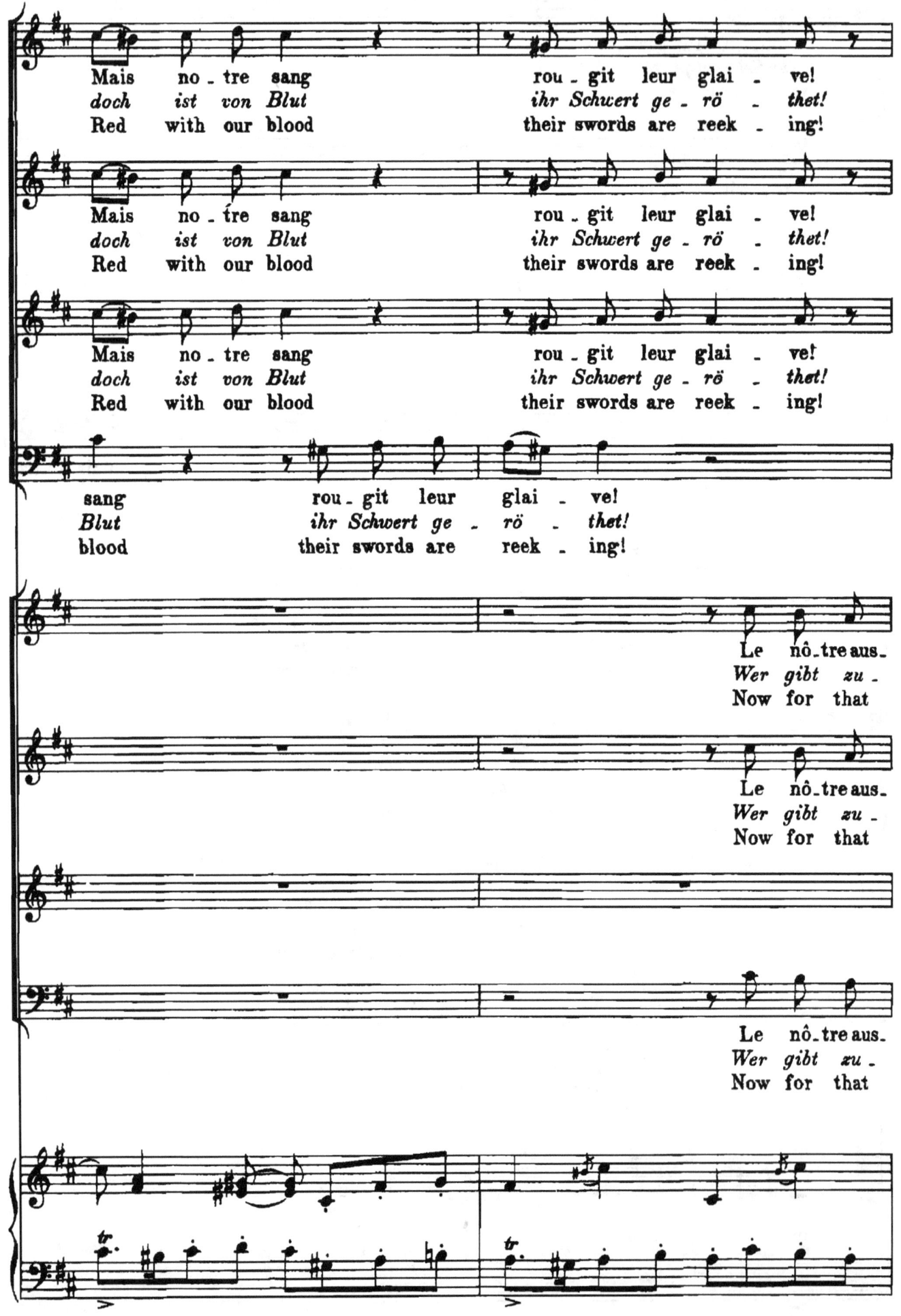

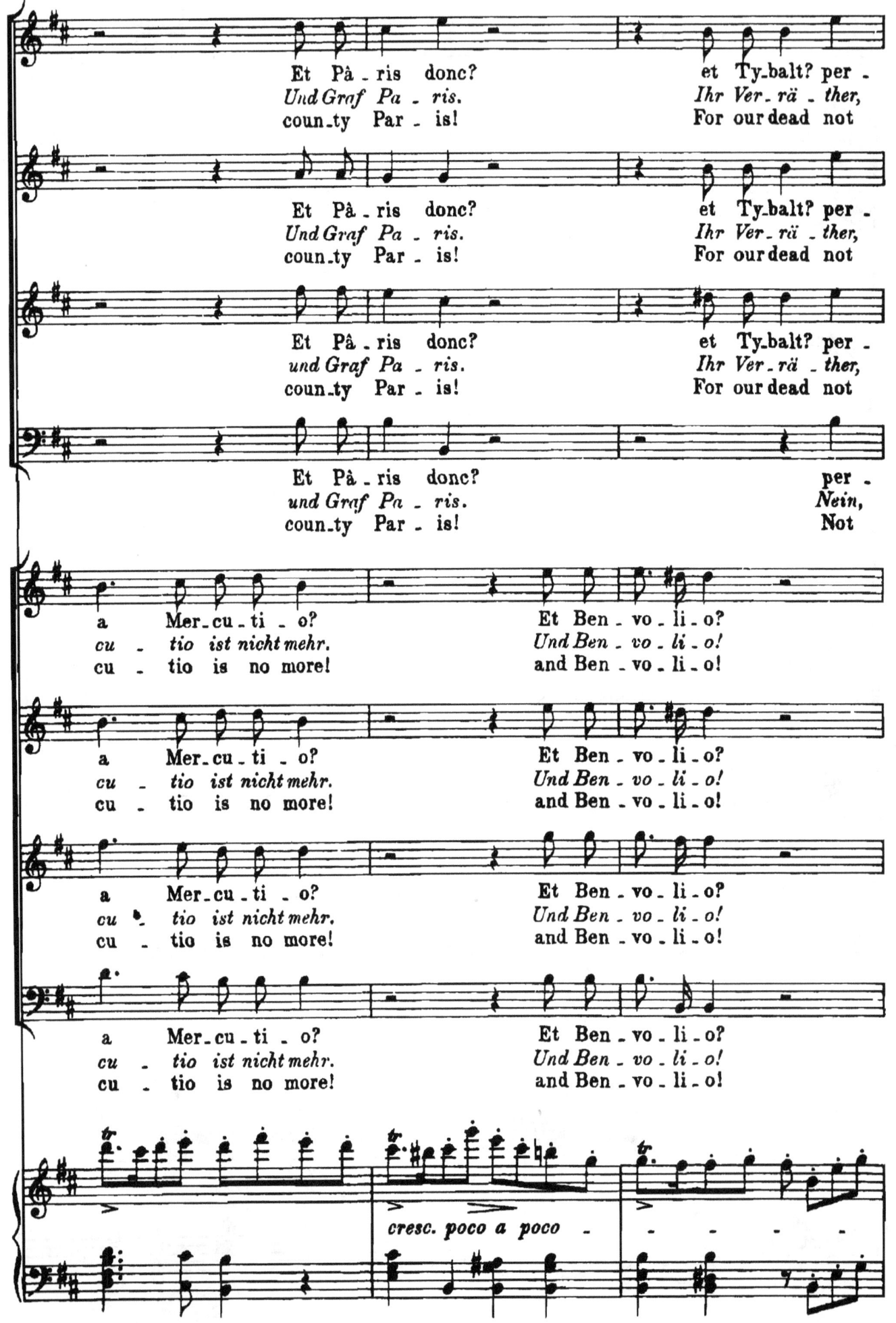

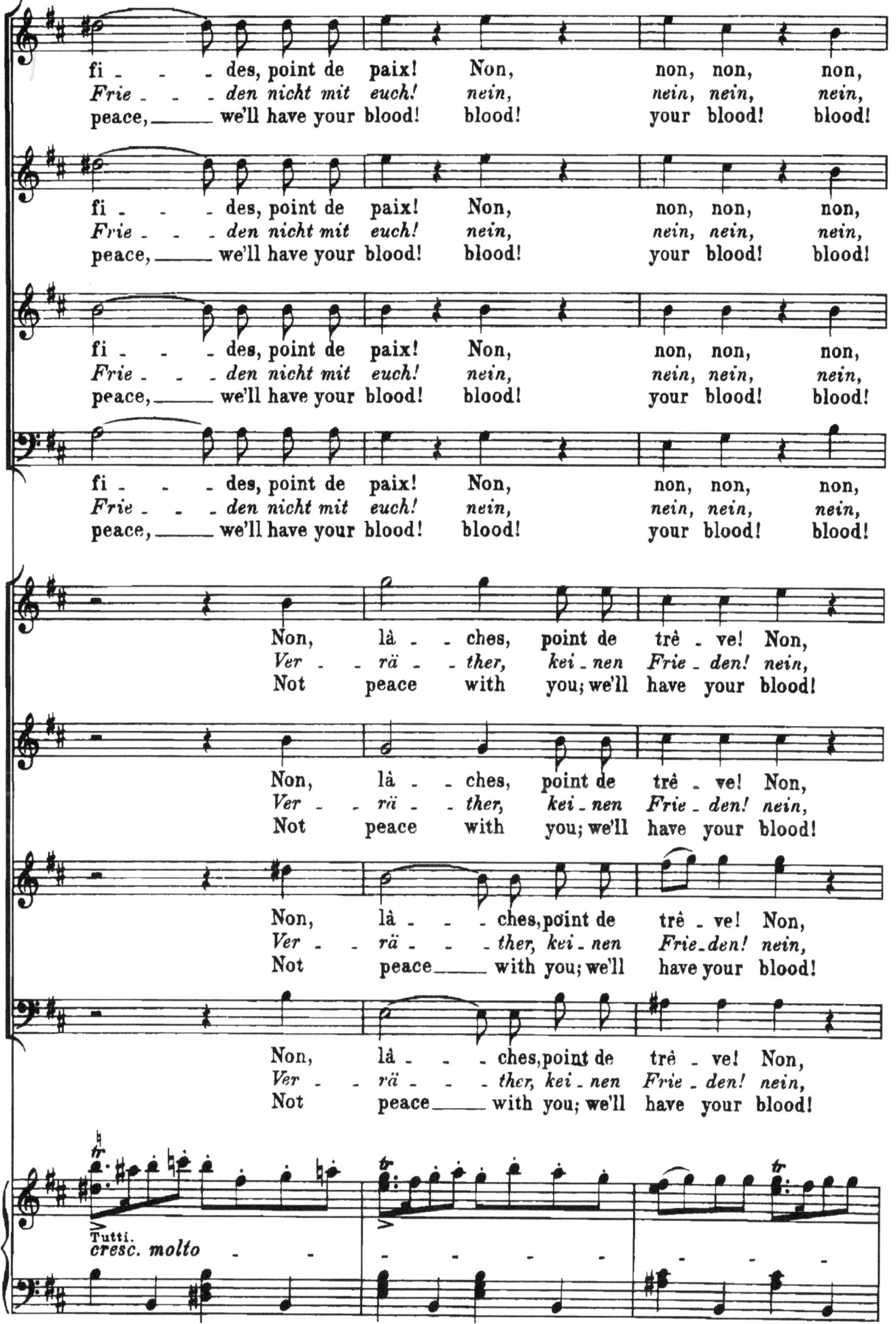

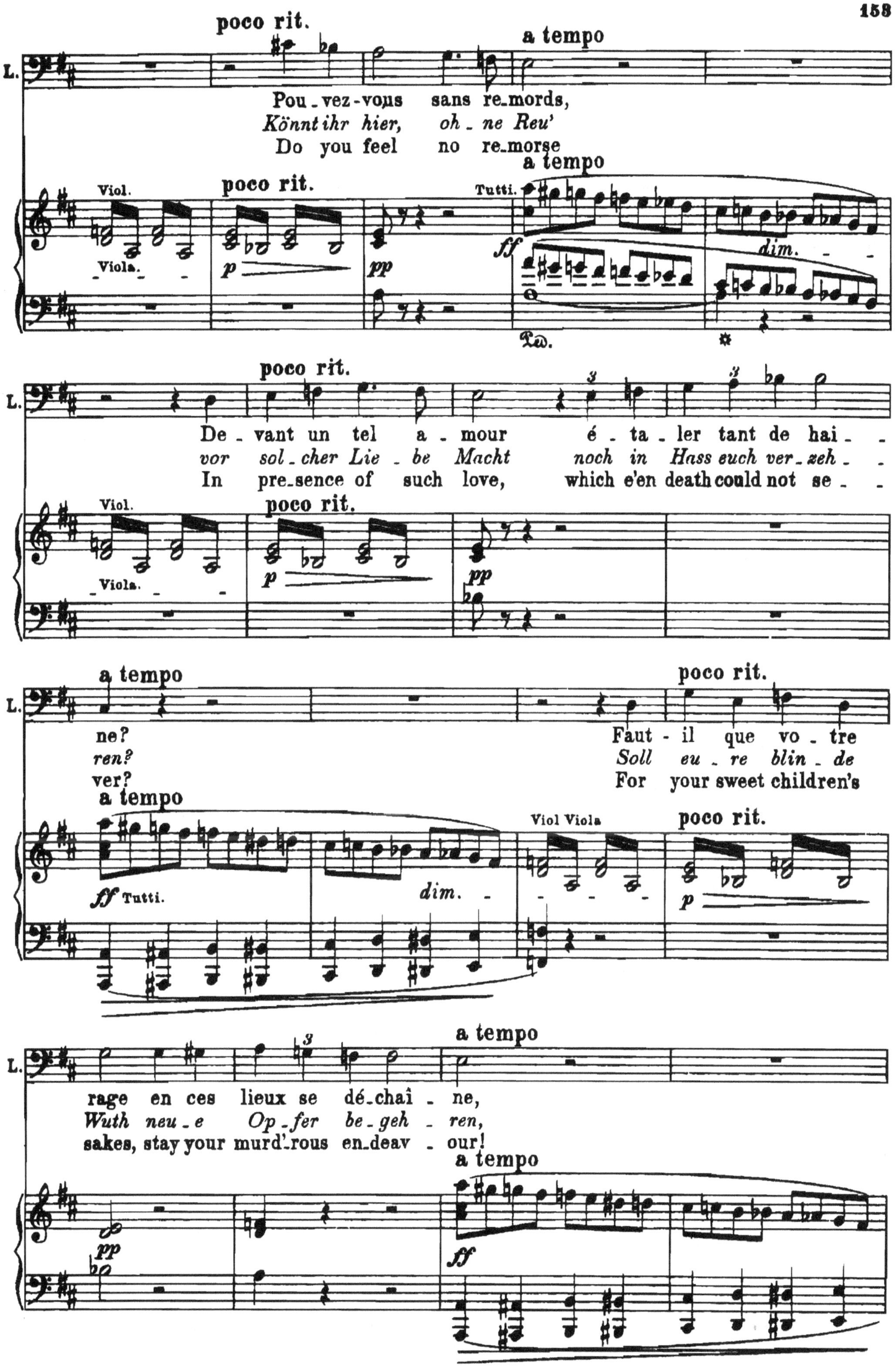
poco rit.
a tempo
L.
Pou - vez - vous sans re - mords,
Könnt ihr hier, oh - ne Reu'
Do you feel no re - morse
Viol.
Viola.
p
pp
Tutti.
ff
dim.
poco rit.
De - vant un tel a - mour é - ta - ler tant de hai -
vor sol - cher Lie - be Macht noch in Hass euch ver - zeh -
In pre - sence of such love, which e'en death could not se -
ne?
ren?
ver?
Faut - il que vo - tre
Soll eu - re blin - de
For your sweet children's
Viol Viola
rage en ces lieux se dé - chaî - ne,
Wuth neu - e Op - fer be - geh - ren,
sakes, stay your murd'rous en - deav - our!

160

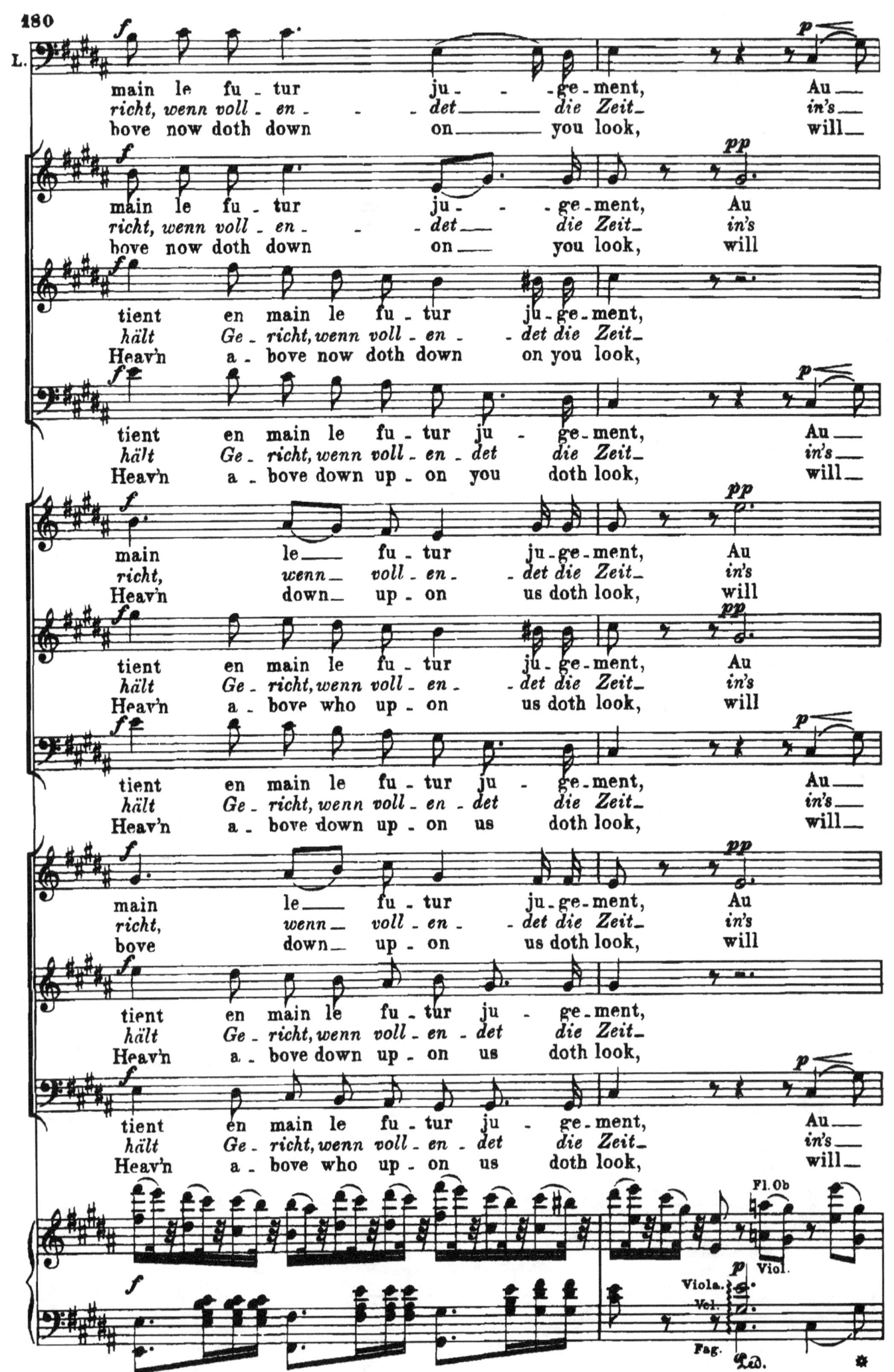

Sur le corps de la fille et sur le corps du fils, Par ce
schwö- ret hier bei des Sohn's und bei der Toch-ter Grab, euch in
By the corse of your daugh-ter and by your son's remains; on the

Sur le corps de la fille et sur le corps du fils, Par ce
schwö- ret hier bei des Sohn's und bei der Toch-ter Grab, euch in
By the corse of your daugh-ter and by your son's remains; on the

corps de la fille et sur le corps du fils, Par ce
hier bei des Sohn's und bei der Toch-ter Grab, euch in
corse of your daugh-ter and by your son's remains; on the

Sur le corps de la fille et sur le corps du fils, Par ce
schwö- ret hier bei des Sohn's und bei der Toch-ter Grab, euch in
By the corse of your daugh-ter and by your son's remains; on the

corps de la fille et sur le corps du fils, Par ce
wir bei des Sohn's und bei der Toch-ter Grab, uns in
corse of your daugh-ter and by your son's remains; on the

Sur le corps de la fille et sur le corps du fils, Par ce
schwö- ren wir bei des Sohn's und bei der Toch-ter Grab, uns in
By the corse of your daugh-ter and by your son's remains; on the

Sur le corps de la fille et sur le corps du fils, Par ce
schwö- ren wir bei des Sohn's und bei der Toch-ter Grab, uns in
By the corse of our daugh-ter and by our son's remains; on the

corps de la fille et sur le corps du fils, Par ce
wir bei des Sohn's und bei der Toch-ter Grab, uns in
corse of our daugh-ter and by our son's remains; on the

corps de la fille et sur le corps du fils, Par ce
wir bei des Sohn's und bei der Toch-ter Grab, uns in
corse of our daugh-ter and by our son's remains; on the

Sur le corps de la fille et sur le corps du fils, Par ce
schwö- ren wir bei des Sohn's und bei der Toch-ter Grab, uns in
By the corse of our daugh-ter and by our son's remains; on the

www.ingramcontent.com/pod-product-compliance
Lightning Source LLC
Chambersburg PA
CBHW081347160426
43200CB00013B/2704